Developing S

DEVELOPING SCIENTIFIC SKILLS AND KNOWLEDGE

year
5

Christine Moorcroft

A & C BLACK

Contents

Introduction   4

Notes on the activities   5

Keeping healthy

The food folk   14
Understanding that to stay healthy we need an
adequate and varied diet

Scurvy at sea   15
Understanding how a scientific idea can be tested

You are what you eat   16
Presenting information about diet and health

Fit for life   17
Recognising that we need exercise to stay healthy
and to maintain our muscles

Feel the beat   18
Learning how to measure pulse rate and relate it
to heart beat

Pulse change   19
Identifying factors that could affect pulse rate and
making predictions about these changes

Drug watch   20
Understanding that substances like tobacco,
alcohol and other drugs can affect the way the
body functions and these effects can be harmful

Life cycles

Travelling seeds: 1   21
Understanding that seeds can be dispersed in a
variety of ways

Travelling seeds: 2   22
Understanding that seeds can be dispersed in a
variety of ways

Wake up seeds!   23
Recognising that plants reproduce; that seeds need
water and warmth (but not light) for germination

Flower power   24
Understanding that insects pollinate some flowers

All about plants   25
Learning about the life cycles of flowering plants

Plant story   26
Learning about the life cycles of flowering plants

The cycle of life   27
Understanding that adults have young and that
these grow into adults which in turn produce young

Gases around us

Solid, liquid or gas?   2
Recognising differences between solids, liquids
and gases

As heavy as air   2
Understanding that air has weight and is all
around us

Air holes   3
Recognising that sponges are solid materials with
air in the 'gaps' in between particles

Soaking in   3
Understanding that soils have air trapped
within them

Where does it go?   3
Recognising that gases are formed when
liquids evaporate

Where does it come from?   3
Making observations and explaining phenomena in
terms of scientific knowledge and understanding

Test it   3
Planning a fair test to evaluate explanations

Changing state

What do you know?   3
Reviewing understanding of solids, liquids and gases

Water, water everywhere   3
Understanding that evaporation is when a liquid
turns to a gas

Drying up   3
Turning ideas into a form that can be investigated,
making a prediction and deciding what evidence to
collect

Washday: 1   3
Explaining everyday examples of 'drying' in terms
of factors affecting evaporation

Washday: 2   3
Constructing a fair test; making careful
measurements

Into the air   4
Recognising that liquids other than water evaporate

What a pong!   4
Recognising that liquids other than water evaporate

The strongest pong   4
Making careful observations and drawing
conclusions; explaining conclusions in terms of
scientific knowledge and understanding

On the boil   4
Understanding that the boiling temperature of
water is 100 °C

Round and round 44
Understanding that water evaporates from oceans, seas and lakes, condenses as clouds and eventually falls as rain

Earth, Sun and Moon

Flat Earth 45
Recognising that the Earth is approximately spherical

Heavenly spheres 46
Recognising that the Earth, Sun and Moon are approximately spherical

Moving Sun 47
Understanding that the Sun appears to move across the sky over the course of a day; that it is the Earth that moves, not the Sun

Fun in the sun 48
Understanding that the Earth spins on its axis once every 24 hours

Rise and shine 49
Understanding that the Sun rises in the general direction of the East and sets in the general direction of the West

A year under the Sun 50
Understanding that the Earth takes a year to make one complete orbit of the Sun, spinning as it goes

Moonrise 51
Understanding that the Earth spins on its axis once every 24 hours

Moonwatch 52
Understanding that the Moon takes approximately 28 days to orbit the Earth

Moon quiz 53
Understanding that the different appearance of the Moon over 28 days provides evidence for a 28-day cycle

Changing sounds

Feel that sound 54
Understanding that sounds are made when objects or materials vibrate

Into your ears 55
Understanding that vibrations from sound sources travel through different materials to the ear

Travelling sounds 56
Making careful observations to identify the types of material through which sound travels

Soundproofers: 1 57
Recognising that some materials prevent vibrations from sound sources reaching the ear

Soundproofers: 2 58
Deciding whether results support or do not support the prediction

High and low 59
Understanding that the word 'pitch' describes how high or low a sound is

Pitch change 60
Understanding that sounds can be made by air vibrating

Enquiry in environmental and technological contexts

Down to earth: 1 61
Asking scientific questions; planning how to answer questions

Down to earth: 2 62
Collecting and recording data appropriately

Down to earth: 3 63
Identifying and describing patterns in data

Down to earth: 4 64
Trying to explain results using scientific knowledge and understanding

Reprinted 2006, 2007
Published 2004 by A & C Black Publishers Limited
38 Soho Square, London W1D 3HB
www.acblack.com

ISBN 978-0-7136-6644-1

Copyright text © Christine Moorcroft, 2004
Copyright illustrations © David Benham, 2004
Copyright cover illustration © Kay Widdowson, 2004
Editor: Jane Klima
Design: Susan McIntyre

The author and publishers would like to thank Catherine Yemm, Trevor Davies and the staff of Balsall Common Primary School for their assistance in producing this series of books.

A CIP catalogue record for this book is available from the British Library.

Printed in Great Britain by St Edmundsbury Press Ltd, Bury St Edmunds, Suffolk.

A & C Black uses paper produced with elemental chlorine-free pulp, harvested from managed sustainable forests.

Introduction

Developing Science is a series of seven photocopiable activity books for science lessons. Each book provides a range of activities that not only develop children's knowledge and understanding of science, but also provide opportunities to develop their scientific skills: planning experimental work, and obtaining and considering evidence.

The activities vary in their approach: some are based on first-hand observation, some present the findings of investigations for the children to analyse and others require the children to find information from books and electronic sources. They focus on different parts of a scientific investigation: questioning, responding to questions, generating ideas, planning, predicting, carrying out a fair test or an investigation, recording findings, checking and questioning findings, explaining findings and presenting explanations.

The activities in **Year 5** are based on Science in the National Curriculum and the QCA scheme of work for Year 5. They provide opportunities for the children to:

- develop curiosity about the things they observe and experience, and explore the world about them with all their senses;
- use this experience to develop their understanding of key scientific ideas and make links between different phenomena and experiences;
- begin to think about models to represent things they cannot directly experience;
- try to make sense of phenomena, seeking explanations and thinking critically about claims and ideas;
- acquire and refine the practical skills needed to investigate questions safely;
- develop skills of predicting, asking questions, making inferences, concluding and evaluating (based on evidence and understanding), and to use these skills in investigative work;
- practise mathematical skills such as counting, ordering numbers, measuring using standard and non-standard measures, and recording and interpreting simple charts;
- learn why numerical and mathematical skills are useful and helpful to understanding;
- think creatively about science and enjoy trying to make sense of phenomena;
- develop language skills through talking about their work and presenting their own ideas, using systematic writing of different kinds;
- use scientific and mathematical language (including technical vocabulary and conventions) and to draw pictures, diagrams and charts to communicate scientific ideas;
- read non-fiction and extract information from sources such as reference books or CD-ROMs;
- work with others, listening to their ideas and treating these with respect;
- develop respect for evidence and critically evaluate ideas which may or may not fit the evidence available;
- develop a respect for the environment and living things and for their own health and safety.

The activities are carefully linked with the National Literacy Strategy to give the children opportunities to develop their reading skills in finding information (for example, scanning text and reading instructions) and to use a range of writing skills in presenting their findings (for example, making notes and writing reports). Science-related vocabulary to introduce is provided in the **Notes on the activities** on pages 5–13.

Teachers are encouraged to introduce the activities presented in this book in a stimulating classroom environment that provides facilities for the children to explore the topics to be covered: for example, through the provision of materials, equipment, pictures, books and electronic sources connected with subjects such as human health, the reproduction of plants and the solar system.

Each activity sheet specifies the learning outcome and has a **Teachers' note** at the foot of the page, which you may wish to mask before photocopying. Expanded teaching notes are provided in the **Notes on the activities**. Most activities also end with a challenge (**Now try this!**), which reinforces the children's learning and provides the teacher with an opportunity for assessment. These activities might be appropriate for only a few children; it is not expected that the whole class should complete them. The extension activities should be completed in a notebook or on a separate sheet of paper.

Health and safety

Developing Science recognises the importance of safety in science lessons and provides advice on the ways in which teachers can make their lessons as safe as possible (including links to useful websites). The books also suggest ways in which to encourage children to take appropriate responsibility for their own safety. Teachers are recommended to follow the safety guidelines provided in the QCA scheme of work or in *Be Safe!* (available from the Association for Science Education – see their website, www.ase.org.uk). Specific health and safety advice is included in the **Notes on the activities** and warnings to the children feature on the activity sheets where relevant.

Online resources

In addition to the photocopiable activity sheets in this book, a collection of online science resources is available on the A & C Black website at www.acblack.com/developingscience. These activities can be used either as stand-alone teaching resources or in conjunction with the printed sheets. An **ICT** icon on an activity page indicates that there is a resource on the website specifically designed to complement that activity.

The website tasks have been designed to provide experiences that are not easy to reproduce in the classroom: for example, observing how plants disperse their seeds.

The notes below expand upon those provided at the foot of the activity pages. They give ideas and suggestions for making the most of the activity sheet, including suggestions for the whole-class introduction, the plenary session or for follow-up work using an adapted version of the sheet. To help teachers to select appropriate learning experiences for their pupils, the activities are grouped into sections according to topic, but the pages need not be presented in the order in which they appear unless stated otherwise. Where appropriate, links to other areas of the curriculum are indicated, in particular, links to literacy and numeracy.

Keeping healthy

This section builds on **Teeth and eating** from **Year 3** and **Moving and growing** from **Year 4**. These activities help the children to learn about the many aspects of keeping healthy: how the muscles work and how exercise affects them, the different foods we need and the substances that can harm us.

CT **The food folk** (page 14) helps the children to understand the meaning of 'a healthy diet'. It is important that the children realise that there are many different types of healthy diet. Ask them if they think there are 'healthy' and 'unhealthy' foods, and point out that we need many different types of food and that foods are not 'bad' or 'good' for us, but that there are some types of food that we need more of than others. *Suggested answers:* It is a good idea to eat fruit every day because it is rich in vitamins and minerals, which keep the body healthy; we need to eat fat (but not too much) – fat is not a 'bad' food: it provides stored energy, which the body uses in many ways, including for keeping warm; fish and meat are good for helping the body to grow and repair itself, but we do not *have* to eat them – there are other foods that work in similar ways (for example, beans and pulses, nuts, eggs and cheese); we should drink plenty of water because the body needs it to keep most parts healthy (our bodies are made up of many materials, but mainly water). This sheet could be related to work in literacy: the children could write advertising slogans and jingles for the food folk'. A complementary activity for this sheet is available on the website (see Year 5 Activity 1).

> **Vocabulary:** *action, diet, energy, growth, mineral, repair, vitamin.*

Scurvy at sea (page 15) helps the children to understand how people can test scientific ideas and underlines the importance of certain foods in our diets. Explain that scurvy is a disease which damages the body's blood vessels. Its symptoms are widespread bruising, bleeding gums and anaemia (reduction in red blood cells). After the children have completed the activity sheet, ask them what differences they identified between life at home and life at

Ensure that the children understand that, although certain foods are rich in vitamins, they should not overeat them. Help them to find out the recommended daily intakes and how much of each vitamin is provided by how much of a food.

sea, and point out that people in the fifteenth century knew a lot less about the effects of diet than we do now. Introduce the idea that diseases can be caused by poor diet, and ask the children why they think going to sea should have brought on a disease caused by a lack of fruit and vegetables in the diet (ships had to stock up before a voyage and often sailed for a long time before they reached ports where they could collect fresh food; a deficiency of vitamin C causes scurvy and vitamin C, unlike some other vitamins, cannot be stored or manufactured by the body). Tell the children about the work of James Lind who, in 1753, was the first person to identify the cause of scurvy, although others had begun to notice that feeding the sufferers on fruits such as lemons, oranges and limes was effective. The following websites are useful:
www.bbc.co.uk/history/discovery/exploration/captaincook_scurvy_01.shtml
www.blupete.com/Hist/Gloss/Scurvy.htm
www.mc.vanderbilt.edu/biolib/hc/journeys/scurvy.html
You could link this with literacy: ask the children to write questions about the discovery of the causes and treatments of scurvy. They could make notes on the main findings of James Lind's reports, which will help them to answer their questions.

> **Resources:** books and leaflets with information about vitamins and deficiency diseases ● a computer

> **Vocabulary:** *cure, deficiency, disease, prevention, scurvy, vitamin C.*

ICT **You are what you eat** (page 16) focuses on the need for variation in our diets. Remember however that children do not have a great deal of choice about what they eat. Ensure that they are not made to feel that their diet at home is not healthy. After completing this activity they could make displays of groups of foods: fatty/oily foods, starchy/sugary foods, protein foods (for growth) and foods rich in minerals and vitamins. You could also introduce the importance of water in the diet and the children could make a display of foods containing a lot of water; in addition to drinks, they should include fruits such as melons, pineapples and oranges. This page provides an opportunity to develop the children's literacy skills in a meaningful context. They could write the names of fruits that are compound words and notice how this helps with their spelling: *blackberry, blueberry, grapefruit, pineapple, strawberry* and so on. A complementary activity for this sheet is available on the website (see Year 5 Activity 2).

> **Resources:** leaflets giving information about nutrition, from food shops, pharmacies, doctors' surgeries ● websites such as BBC Health (www.bbc.co.uk/health)

> **Vocabulary:** *diet, fat, mineral, oil, protein, starch, sugar, vitamin.*

Fit for life (page 17) encourages the children to think about the effects of different types of exercise. They will be aware of some of the muscles they use, such as

Emphasise the dangers of straining muscles. The children should not push themselves too hard when exercising.

those in the arms and legs, but point out others such as those in the back and shoulders – and point out that any exercise makes the heart and lungs work harder (ask them how they can tell).

> **Vocabulary:** *breathing, exercise, heart, lungs, muscles.*

Feel the beat (page 18) shows the children how to measure the effects of exercise on their pulse rate and to record these measurements on a chart. They also learn to relate pulse rate to heart beat and develop an understanding of the importance of repeating measurements to check them for accuracy. The children who complete the extension activity, which draws attention to the relationship between pulse and heart beat, could share their ideas with the rest of the class. One way of listening to heart beats, in order to count them, is for a child to place his or her head on someone's chest, to use a stethoscope or to use a home-made stethoscope made from a funnel attached to rubber tubing. They could also record their heart beats by placing the microphone of a cassette recorder on their chest and recording it on full volume. The advantage of a recorded heart beat is that an adult can help the children to count and check the beats accurately.

> **Resources:** a stopwatch or seconds timer

> **Vocabulary:** *beat, heart, pulse.*

Pulse change (page 19) develops the children's understanding of the effects of different types of exercise on the pulse/heart. They learn how a scientific question can be turned into a form that can

 The children should exercise normally, as in PE lessons, and should not try to test their stamina.

be investigated and how to record the results of their investigation on a bar chart. Encourage them to predict the changes in their pulse rate after different types of exercise and to say if they think the length of time they exercise will affect their pulse rate. Do they think it will continue to increase if they exercise for longer? After the activity discuss why the pulse/heart rate should increase after exercise; help the children to relate their results to their observations of what happens to their bodies after exercise (faster breathing, hotness, sweating). Muscles use oxygen as they convert energy from food into movement (and into heat, as a by-product). Oxygen is taken into the body in the air we breathe into our lungs. Blood vessels carry blood containing oxygen from the lungs to the heart from where it is pumped around the muscles. The oxygen is used up and the blood returns to the heart and then back to the lungs to collect more oxygen. Encourage the children to use appropriate spelling strategies for difficult words such as *muscle* and *oxygen*. Also link this work with mathematics (handling data).

> **Resources:** a stopwatch or seconds timer

> **Vocabulary:** *beat, exercise, heart, increase, pulse, raise.*

Drug watch (page 20) develops the children's knowledge about drugs: that substances such as alcohol, tobacco and other drugs can affect the way in which the body functions and can be

 Do not use 'smoking machine' demonstrations that show the effects of cigarettes, because tar is carcinogenic.

harmful; that medicines are drugs and usually have helpful effects on the body although they can have side-effects and misuse can be harmful. Teachers need to be sensitive to the activities of the children's families in relation to drugs. Provide leaflets from health centres and pharmacies and access to websites that provide accurate, balanced information. Useful websites include:
BBC Health: www.bbc.co.uk/health
Drug Information Online: www.drugs.com
Health Education Board for Scotland:
www.hebs.com/topics/smoking/index.htm
www.hebs.com/topics/alcohol/index.htm
www.hebs.com/topics/drugs/index.htm
Department of Health UK: www.doh.gov.uk
NHS Direct: www.nhsdirect.nhs.uk

> **Vocabulary:** *alcohol, aspirin, drug, heroin, medicine, tobacco.*

Life cycles

The activities in this section develop the children's understanding about plant and animal reproduction and life cycles. They build on **Plants and animals** and **Health and growth** from **Year 2** and **Helping plants grow well** from **Year 3**.

 Travelling seeds: 1 (page 21) helps the children to understand how and why plants disperse their seeds and how the structure of seeds aids their particular form of dispersal. Tell the children that the seeds from a plant would have to fight for survival if they all landed in the same spot and that to help the seeds to survive the plant disperses

> Seeds taken from flowers or fruits are safer than those bought for planting, which are usually treated with fungicides. Avoid nuts, in case any children are allergic to them. Remind the children that some seeds are poisonous and that they should keep their hands away from their faces after handling the seeds.

them. Begin by discussing a familiar seed such as sycamore; ask the children how it moves away from the tree on which it grows and discuss how the structure of the seed helps it to travel through the air. Show them other airborne seeds (or pictures of them): columbine, dandelion, grasses, poppy, rosebay willowherb, thistle; seeds dispersed by animals (either by passing through their digestive systems – for example, berries, fruits and nuts – or by attaching themselves to animal fur by burrs – for example, agrimony, burdock, teasel, water avens); waterborne seeds, which float: coconut, lotus, sea rocket; and seeds that are spread when their pods explode and fling them out: meadow cranesbill, lupin, policeman's helmet, sweet pea. Ask the children to notice the special features of the seed and to think about how it can be dispersed. Is it hollow (enabling it to float)? Is it in a pod (which can explode)? Is it small and light or with wings or parachutes (to enable it to be scattered by the wind)? Is it attractive to birds and other animals as a food? Or does it have hooks (to attach itself to fur)? The children could begin a database of plants that includes information about their size, structure, leaves, flowers and seeds. A complementary activity for this page and for page 22 is available on the website (see Year 5 Activity 3).

> **Resources:** examples (or pictures) of seeds that are dispersed in different ways

> **Vocabulary:** *airborne, digestive system, disperse, explode, seed, waterborne.*

CT **Travelling seeds: 2** (page 22) encourages the children to use what they have learned about seed dispersal and how the structure of a seed helps in its dispersal. After the activity, ask them to explain how they decided in which groups to place the seeds. *Answers:* Dispersed by wind: ash, cedar, columbine, couch grass, fir, poppy, Scots pine, sycamore, thistle, timothy grass; dispersed by animals (eaten): apple, beech, cherry, cotoneaster, fig, oak, redcurrant, rowan, strawberry, yew; (carried on animals' fur): burdock, teasel; dispersed by explosion: laburnum, lupin; dispersed by water: coconut, sea rocket, yellow iris. You could challenge the children to find out how the invention of Velcro arose from the observation of burrs attaching themselves to a dog's hair. A complementary activity for this page and for page 21 is available on the website (see Year 5 Activity 3).

Resources: books such as *The Naturetrail Omnibus* (Usborne), *Trees* (Usborne), *Wild Flowers* (Usborne) and *Eyewitness Plant* (Dorling Kindersley)

> **Vocabulary:** *airborne, digestive system, disperse, explode, seed, waterborne.*

Wake up seeds! (page 23) develops the children's understanding of how plants reproduce and about the conditions needed for germination. They are asked to consider those conditions and to plan how to test them, altering one factor at a time so that their tests are fair. It is important to point out that germination is not the same as growth and that the conditions required for each part of the plant's development are slightly different. Encourage the children to discuss the information in the seeds fact-file and to consider what they can deduce from it: for example, seeds germinate in the spring and not in the autumn when they first land on the ground; this suggests that the seeds are not ready to germinate immediately and that when they are ready to germinate they need warmth. The children should find that seeds germinate when they have water and warmth but that light is not needed for germination. To link this with literacy, focus on the formation of words ending in *-ation: fertilisation, germination, pollination.*

Resources: potting compost or soil from dog- and cat-free areas ● plant pots or trays ● old spoons ● quick-germinating seeds such as broad beans, cress, marigold, radish or tomato

> **Vocabulary:** *dormant, germinate, grow, light, seed, warmth, water.*

Flower power (page 24) introduces pollination and why it is necessary. Provide a flower whose male and female parts can easily be identified, such as a buttercup or mallow, and diagrams of flowers to help them to recognise these parts and to learn the names of them. Explain that the seeds grow from ovules in the female part of the flower once the ovules have been fertilised by pollen from the male part. Some flowers have only male or only female parts; in some species the two different types of flower grow on the same plant, or they might grow on separate plants. Explain how insects such as bees and butterflies can pollinate flowers by carrying pollen on their bodies from one

 The children should avoid touching their faces when handling plants and should wash their hands afterwards. Take care with pollen: some children (for example, hayfever sufferers) might be allergic to it and it can stain clothes.

flower to another. Children who undertake the extension activity should become aware of the importance of the shapes, patterns and colours of flowers; some patterns attract insects to the centre of the flower where the stamens and stigmas are, others have shapes into which insects such as bees have to crawl in order to collect nectar – at the same time pollen brushes on to the hairs on their bodies and is deposited in the next flower they visit. Develop the children's spelling skills by encouraging them to notice spellings that appear inconsistent: for example, *pollen/pollination*. They could think of others from other subjects: for example, *aqualung/aqueduct*.

Resources: a buttercup or mallow flower ● magnifying glasses

> **Vocabulary:** *fertilisation, fertilise, ovary, ovule, petal, pollen, pollinate, stamen, stigma.*

All about plants (page 25) consolidates the children's learning about the pollination of plants and the germination and dispersal of seeds, and helps them to learn the vocabulary associated with these. The glossary links with the development of literacy skills and the use of those skills for a purpose.

> **Vocabulary:** *dispersal, disperse, dormant, fertilisation, fertilise, germinate, germination, ovary, ovule, petal, pollen, pollinate, seed, stamen, stigma.*

Plant story (page 26) helps the children to understand the life cycle of flowering plants, including pollination, fertilisation, seed dispersal and germination. They could collect pictures of plants at different stages in their development and make a labelled display of plant life cycles.

> **Vocabulary:** *dispersal, disperse, dormant, fertilisation, fertilise, germinate, germination, ovary, ovule, petal, pollen, pollinate, seed, stamen, stigma.*

The cycle of life (page 27) helps the children to understand the life cycle of humans and other mammals and to notice similarities and differences between them. They could first sort a collection of photographs of people into sets according to their stage of development. Each group could agree on a way of grouping the pictures they have and display them, glued on to large sheets of paper. Ask them to justify the way in which they have grouped the pictures and to define babyhood, childhood, adolescence and adulthood. Some children might be able to divide adulthood further (for example, child-bearing age, middle age, old age). With the children who undertake the extension activity, discuss what is meant by *gestation*.

> **Vocabulary:** *adolescence, adulthood, babyhood, childhood, gestation.*

Gases around us

The activities in this section develop the children's knowledge and understanding about the properties of gases. They learn that materials can be in three states (solid, liquid or gas) and that each has distinctive characteristics. They also learn that air is a gas consisting of a mixture of gases and that gases can be useful in everyday life. The activities build on the children's previous learning in **Rocks and soils** from **Year 3** and **Solids, liquids and how they can be separated** and **Friction** from **Year 4**.

Discuss any everyday solids, liquids and gases that can be dangerous, such as household cleaning powders, ice taken straight from the freezer (it can stick to the skin), firelighters, petrol, paraffin, household cleaning liquids such as bleach, domestic mains gas, bottled gas (in liquid form in the bottles) and the gases used in aerosols. Point out that some gases are poisonous when inhaled; gases might also be explosive or flammable. The children could research harmful solids, liquids and gases during another lesson or for homework.

ICT **Solid, liquid or gas?** (page 28) revises the children's previous learning about solids and liquids and encourages them to think about the nature of the materials around them. After they have completed the activity, invite them to read from their lists; the others should listen and comment on any differences between those and their own lists. You could link this with their previous learning about breathing: like other animals, we breathe in air in order to obtain the oxygen our bodies need; animals die if they are starved of oxygen or if they breathe in poisonous gases. Discuss the differences between the behaviour of solids, liquids and gases and help the children to compile a checklist for identifying the state of a material:

State of material	Characteristics
Solid	It can be piled up. It keeps its shape when taken out of a container. It cannot be poured unless it is in many pieces. It cannot flow through tubes or pipes. If you put it on a level surface such as a table-top, it does not run off. If you make a hole in the bottom of a container of solid, the solid stays inside unless it is in small pieces which can fit through the hole. If you open the top of a container of solid, the solid stays inside it. If you tip it out of a container, it falls downwards.
Liquid	It cannot be piled up. It does not keep its shape unless it is in a container. It can be poured. It can flow through tubes or pipes. If you put it on a level surface such as a table-top, it runs off. If you make a hole in the bottom of a container of liquid, the liquid runs downwards. If you open the top of a container of liquid, the liquid stays inside it. If you tip it out of a container, it falls downwards.
Gas	It cannot be piled up. It does not keep its shape when taken out of a container. It cannot be poured. It can flow through tubes or pipes. You cannot put it on a level surface such as a table-top because it escapes in all directions. If you make a hole in the bottom of a container of gas, the gas escapes in all directions. If you open the top of a container of gas, the gas escapes in all directions. If you let it out of a container, it goes in all directions.

To develop literacy skills in a meaningful context, you could ask the children to devise a flow chart to explain what happens when a solid, a liquid and a gas are released from containers, and why. A complementary activity for this sheet is available on the website (see Year 5 Activity 4).

Vocabulary: *aerosol, air, carbon dioxide, gas, helium, liquid, petrol, solid.*

As heavy as air (page 29) develops the children's understanding that air has weight and is all around us. They have opportunities to explain observed phenomena related to air Do not allow children to inflate balloons by mouth.

in terms of their scientific knowledge and understanding. Ask the children to name objects that usually contain air; introduce others, including inflated balloons, bread, cakes, balls and squeaky toys. Would they be lighter or heavier if they did not contain air? Everyday ideas are sometimes at odds with scientific knowledge: cakes are said to be light if they contain air (they are lighter cooked than uncooked because they lose moisture although they gain air).

Resources: wire coat-hangers ● balloons ● string ● balloon pumps

Vocabulary: *air, balance, heavier, heavy, inflate, light, lighter, weigh.*

Air holes (page 30) promotes understanding that 'empty' containers have air in them unless the air has been sucked out. The children learn that sponges are solid materials with air holes and they are encouraged to make careful observations of materials and to explain these observations using scientific knowledge and understanding. Discuss what forces the air out of the objects when they are put into water.

Resources: bowls of water ● balls (inflatable and sealed) ● balloons ● balloon pumps ● drinks cans ● sponges ● small vases or jugs

Vocabulary: *air, empty, inflate, particles.*

Soaking in (page 31) helps the children to recognise that sand and soil have air trapped inside them; they are asked to measure volumes carefully, to recognise whether their measurements need to be repeated and to use their results to compare the Soil should be from cat- and dog-free areas; the children should keep their hands away from their faces while handling soil and should wash their hands afterwards.

amounts of air trapped in different soils. You could collect samples of different types of soil: sand, sandy soil, clay, peat and loam. Ask the children to use adjectives accurately to describe different soil types; encourage them to use a thesaurus. This page also offers opportunities to develop mathematical skills (measuring volume).

Resources: different types of soil ● clear plastic pots ● magnifying glasses ● measuring cylinders ● measuring jugs

Vocabulary: *air, clay, loam, measuring cylinder, peat, volume.*

Where does it go? (page 32) helps the children to explain the 'disappearance' of water during evaporation and to think of a way to test their ideas. When the Perfume and other sprays should not be sprayed towards the face.

children guess what happened to the disappearing water, accept all their ideas – however imaginative! – before discussing how probable they are. Point out that the best way to test an idea of this kind is to try to prove it is wrong (it is much more difficult to prove that an idea is *right*, although the children can collect evidence to *support* their idea). Their ideas could be linked to other instances of water evaporating: for example, puddles drying up, drying washing, drying hair. Many children think that the water soaks through the saucer (ask them to look underneath the saucer and to say if the water can be seen there and, if not, where it has gone). You could also carry out some practical demonstrations for the children to explain: for example, how does the smell of perfume, disinfectant or air freshener get into their noses? (The liquid evaporates, becoming a gas, and moves through the air into their noses.) This sheet provides practice in writing explanations. Encourage the use of words and phrases such as *as a result, because, in order to, so*.

Resources: a saucer ● water

Vocabulary: *disappear, evaporate, gas, water vapour.*

Where does it come from? (page 33) encourages the children to make observations and to explain them in terms of scientific

Ice cubes should not be handled straight from the freezer.

knowledge and understanding. It provides practice in writing explanations. They learn that there is water in the air in the form of a gas (evaporated water) and that it can turn back to a liquid if it is cooled. You could discuss other examples of condensation: for example, at a swimming pool or on windows. The explanation of the water on the sides of the can seems obvious to adults, but many children think it must come from the ice inside the can (that it somehow gets through the sides of the can). Collect all their explanations and help them to find a way to test them ('If that happens, how could you stop it happening?').

Resources: cans ● ice

Vocabulary: *condensation, condense, evaporate, evaporation, gas, liquid.*

Test it (page 34) develops understanding of condensation and evaporation and encourages the children to plan a fair test to

Ice cubes should not be handled straight from the freezer.

find out if their explanations are correct. Discuss their plans and what they expect to happen if their explanation is wrong and if it is right. To test whether the water on the outside of the can has come from the ice inside it (either through the can or over the top of it) you could colour the water that you freeze to make the ice; to support the explanation that the water comes from the air in the classroom, the children could put the can into an airtight container to stop air from the classroom reaching the outside of the can, add the ice and then close the lid.

Resources: cans ● ice ● plastic boxes ● plastic bags ● food dye

Vocabulary: *condensation, condense, evaporate, evaporation, gas, liquid.*

Changing state

The activities in this section build on **Solids, liquids and how they can be separated** from **Year 3** and **Gases around us** (see above). They consolidate the children's understanding about

reversible changes of state and encourage the children to use their knowledge to explain various phenomena.

What do you know? (page 35) reviews the children's understanding of solids, liquids and gases. It encourages them to take an active part in the assessment of their knowledge and understanding. They can draw lines to link any of the words as long as they write on the line a sentence that links the two words.

Vocabulary: *change, cool, evaporate, flow, freeze, gas, ice, liquid, melt, pour, powder, shape, solid, steam, volume, warm, water.*

Water, water everywhere (page 36) develops the children's awareness that evaporation is when a liquid turns to a gas and encourages them to explain as *evaporation* the 'disappearance' of water in a range of situations. It will be necessary to spread this activity over a week or so – it cannot be completed in a single lesson. Focus on the mathematical skills involved in the accurate measurement and recording of length. After the children have completed the activity, discuss what their findings tell them about the conditions that speed up evaporation. They should notice that dry windy weather is the best for drying up puddles. This is because warm air moves across the surface of the water absorbing particles from its surface.

Resources: string ● chalk ● 2-litre measuring jug ● metre rulers

Vocabulary: *conditions, evaporate, gas, liquid, measurement, observation, prediction.*

Drying up (page 37) helps the children to turn ideas about evaporation into a form that can be investigated, to make predictions and to decide what evidence to collect in order to test their predictions. The children are encouraged to construct a fair test and to make careful measurements. Rather than try to time how long the water takes to dry (which is impractical) the children could place the plastic pot and the saucer containing the same small amounts of water side by side in a place where they can easily be seen. You could ask the children to write non-chronological reports about their investigations.

Resources: 100 ml measuring cylinders ● plastic pots ● saucers ● water

Vocabulary: *dry up, evaporate, gas, liquid, measurement, observation, prediction.*

Washday: 1 and **2** (pages 38–39) encourage the children to explain everyday examples of drying in terms of factors affecting evaporation. They have an opportunity to evaluate an investigation and to improve it, making it a fair test. After they have completed the survey (**Washday: 1**), discuss what makes each a good method of drying washing and identify its advantages and disadvantages. The children could report what people said to them about each method during their survey. The extension activity in **Washday: 2** suggests using sugar paper because it is easy to see when it has dried. The children should use paper of the same size and, to ensure that each is equally wet, they could immerse them in water for the count of 2.

Vocabulary: *dry up, evaporate, factor, fair test, gas, liquid.*

Into the air (page 40) develops the children's knowledge that liquids other than water evaporate. They develop skills in turning their ideas into a form that can be investigated,

Do not allow the children to heat the liquids.

making predictions and deciding what evidence to collect to check their predictions. They are encouraged to make careful observations and draw conclusions, explaining these in terms of scientific knowledge and understanding.

> **Vocabulary:** *evaporate, fair test, gas, liquid, measurement, observation, prediction.*

What a pong! and **The strongest pong** (pages 41–42) reinforce the children's knowledge that liquids other than water evaporate. They are asked to make careful observations and draw conclusions, explaining these in terms of scientific knowledge and understanding. Before the children begin **What a pong!**, let them smell some perfume, and ask

Warn the children never to smell unknown materials unless a trusted adult tells them that this is safe. Do not allow the children to put the perfume on their skin in case of allergies.

them to draw a diagram showing how the smell gets from the bottle to their nose (the perfume begins to evaporate – it becomes a gas – and travels through the air in all directions; some enters their noses, where the sense of smell is stimulated by it).

Resources: some cheap perfumes, colognes and aftershaves ● small dishes ● long tape measures

> **Vocabulary:** *evaporate, measure, observe, predict.*

On the boil (page 43) develops the children's understanding that evaporation is when a liquid turns to a gas. They are asked to make careful observations and draw conclusions, explaining these conclusions in terms of scientific knowledge and understanding. This provides scope for using and developing mathematical skills in taking and recording temperatures, recording time, handling and interpreting data

An adult should heat the water (in a small saucepan or an electric kettle) and read out the temperature after each minute. Hold the thermometer with an oven glove and do not let it touch the base of the pan or the element of the kettle. Ensure that no child is near the hot water.

and working with numbers below zero. Most children predict that the temperature of the water will continue to rise when it is heated, even after it boils. Pure water boils (turns to a gas, or evaporates) at 100 °C. (For this purpose tap water can be used – the temperature reading will be about 100 °C, but if you want strict accuracy, use distilled water.) This is a change of state; changes of state take place at a constant temperature; therefore once the water has reached boiling point it cannot get any hotter, and so the graph will become a straight horizontal line. Before the activity begins, the children could devise their own safety rules; ensure that these include remaining seated throughout the activity.

Resources: small saucepan or electric kettle ● oven gloves ● laboratory (stirring) thermometer with a scale of about –10 °C to 110 °C

> **Vocabulary:** *boil, boiling point, Celsius, change of state, evaporate, gas, measure, observe, predict, temperature, thermometer.*

Round and round (page 44) develops the children's understanding of the water cycle, in particular that evaporation and condensation are changes of state; that they are the opposite of one another and can be reversed. Begin by asking them where tap water comes from. Use videos and other secondary sources (including the Internet) to help the children to learn about how water is brought to buildings, how the quality of drinking water is ensured and where it goes to after it is used. A useful website is www.environment-agency.gov.uk/subjects/waterres/?lang=e.

> **Vocabulary:** *cloud, condensation, condense, evaporate, evaporation, gas, liquid, water cycle.*

Earth, Sun and Moon

The activities in this section develop the children's knowledge and understanding about the shapes and relative sizes of the Earth, Sun and Moon. They learn, through using models, how the three bodies move in relation to one another and how these movements relate to night and day, months and the year. The activities build on **Light and dark** from **Year 1** and **Light and shadows** from **Year 3**. A visit to a planetarium would enrich work on this topic, or you could visit a planetarium website:
England: www.london-planetarium.com
Northern Ireland: www.armagh-planetarium.co.uk
Scotland: www.roe.ac.uk/vc
Wales: www.techniquest.org

Flat Earth (page 45) helps the children to learn that the Earth is approximately spherical, that it is not always possible to collect evidence to test scientific ideas and that the evidence might have to come from secondary sources. Invite one of them to come out and draw the Earth on a chalkboard. The others can check, and correct it if they think it is wrong. How do they know what the Earth looks like? Discuss the sources available: globes, scientific reports, television programmes, films, photographs taken from space and so on. Encourage them to find out from such sources how scientists have found the information to enable them to draw accurate maps and diagrams of the Earth. Useful websites include the London Planetarium (www.london-planetarium.com) and NASA (www.nasa.gov).

Resources: information books ● CD-ROMs ● computer

> **Vocabulary:** *approximately, Earth, roughly, sphere, spherical.*

Heavenly spheres (page 46) develops the children's knowledge about the shapes and relative sizes of the Earth, the Sun and the Moon and about the difficulties in collecting evidence to test

It is dangerous to look directly at the Sun. Its rays can harm the eyes and even cause blindness.

scientific ideas. They will learn that the evidence sometimes has to be collected from secondary sources. Invite the children to talk about what they already know about the sizes and shapes of the Earth, Sun and Moon and to draw concept maps (see page 35). Discuss how they know and where the facts can be checked.

Resources: information books ● CD-ROMs ● computer

> **Vocabulary:** *Earth, Moon, sphere, Sun.*

Moving Sun (page 47) helps the children understand that the Sun looks as if it moves across the sky over the course of a day but, in fact, it is the Earth's rotation on its axis that makes the Sun appear to move. They learn to make observations of where the Sun rises and sets and to recognise the patterns in these observations. It is useful to take the children outside at different times to look at the lengths and directions of the shadows of the school building and to discuss the cause of these changes in relation to the changing position of the Sun. The children could also experiment with torches and models, placing a model person made from Plasticine on a globe, rotating the globe and observing what happens to the model's shadow. Revise the use of a compass to find North, South, East and West, and ask the children in which direction the Sun appears to move across the sky. In connection with the directions North, South, East and West, revise mathematical work on right angles. A complementary activity for this sheet is available on the website (see Year 5 Activity 5).

> It is dangerous to look directly at the Sun. Its rays can harm the eyes and even cause blindness.

Resources: compass

Vocabulary: *axis, rotate, rotation, spin, stationary.*

Fun in the sun (page 48) develops the children's learning about the use of shadows in making clocks. They develop their understanding that the Sun appears to move across the sky over the course of a day, that the Earth spins on its axis once every 24 hours and that it is daytime in the part of the Earth facing the Sun and night-time in the part facing away from the Sun. You could begin by telling the children that before clocks were invented the sundial was one way people could tell the time of day (but not in cloudy weather). Show them a garden sundial on a sunny day and help them to use it (note that during British Summer Time the sundial will be an hour behind the time shown on their watches). You could also make a display of pictures of different types of sundial and help the children to find out how they are used. The children should find that the shadows cast by the end of the cereal box become shorter towards midday and then increase in length. Use a torch and a globe to demonstrate that the part of the Earth facing the Sun has daylight while the part facing away from it is in darkness:

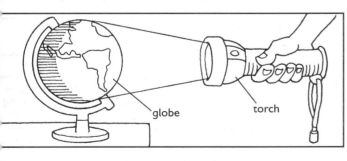

globe   torch

Resources: cereal box ● scissors ● ruler

Vocabulary: *axis, British Summer Time, daylight, rotate, sundial.*

Rise and shine (page 49) consolidates the children's learning that the Sun rises in the general direction of the East and sets in the general direction of the West. They are asked to present times of sunrise and sunset on a graph and to recognise trends

> Warn the children never to look at the Sun.

and patterns in the data. This provides links with work in mathematics (handling and interpreting data and recording time). You could begin by asking the children at about what time it goes dark in the evenings and at about what time in the morning it becomes light. Do they ever get up in the dark or go to bed in daylight? Is it always the same? Tell them that they are going to find out the exact time of sunrise and sunset (you could begin by recording these on a daily basis and then using the activity sheet as a record for a long-term investigation). What patterns do the children notice? They could work out how long daylight lasts and predict whether or not the pattern they notice will continue or if it will change: for example, will sunrise (or sunset) continue to become earlier (or later) each day? A long-term investigation will show this, or the children could look up (in *Whitaker's Almanack*) the times of sunrise and sunset for the same date of each month for the whole year, or find the earliest and latest sunrise and sunset of the year, the 'longest day' (Summer Solstice, 21 June) and the 'shortest day' (Winter Solstice, 21 December).

Resources: a diary that gives sunrise and sunset times ● newspapers ● *Whitaker's Almanack*

Vocabulary: *daylight, lighting-up time, solstice, sunrise, sunset.*

A year under the Sun (page 50) demonstrates that the Earth takes a year to make one complete orbit of the Sun, spinning as it goes, and the children discover the difficulties in finding out about phenomena such as the length of the year using first-hand experience. Invite the children to talk about their understanding of 'a year': how many days are there in a year? Who decided how many days there were in a year, and how? The Earth takes 365.25 days to orbit the Sun. To make the year into a round number of days we count it as 365 and add one day to February every four years (hence 'Leap Years'). Introduce the term *orbit* and use a globe to demonstrate and explain how it is different from *rotation*. The children could contribute to a display about the calendar. This page encourages the children to use information books and electronic sources in an organised way: to consider what they know, what questions this raises and where to find the answers.

Resources: information books and CD-ROMs about the Earth and Sun and about calendars ● a computer ● planetarium websites

Vocabulary: *calendar, date, orbit.*

Moonrise (page 51) reinforces the children's learning that the Earth spins on its axis once every 24 hours. Show them how to use a compass to find South and discuss how they can work out where South is from their homes by noticing directions in which the Sun rises and sets. They should find, if they face South, that the Moon appears to move across the sky from left to right and that it becomes lower in the sky. Point out that, although the Sun appears to (but does not) orbit the Earth, the Moon really does orbit the Earth. Discuss how similar observations can be interpreted differently and how secondary sources are needed to clarify what is happening. Point out that, unlike the Sun, the Moon has no light of its own, but reflects the Sun's light.

Resources: compass

Vocabulary: *direction, East, North, orbit, rotate, South, West.*

In **Moonwatch** (page 52) the children learn about the Moon's orbit of the Earth and about the apparent changes in the shape of the Moon during its 28-day cycle. You could begin by asking the children to draw a picture of the Moon. Invite them to compare their drawings. Are they all the same? If not, why not? Ask the children if they know why the shape of the Moon changes, and use a torch and two balls to demonstrate that the reason why it appears to change shape is that at different times we can see different amounts of the Moon's surface:

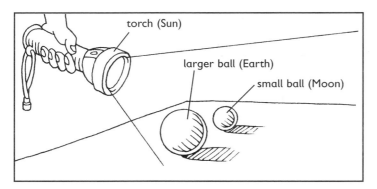

torch (Sun)

larger ball (Earth)

small ball (Moon)

Also use the model to show the children why there is one part of the Moon's surface that we never see (because as the Earth rotates, so does the Moon). Remind the children that, unlike the Sun, the Moon has no light of its own, but we can see it because it reflects the Sun's light. It is safe to look at the Moon.

> **Vocabulary:** *calendar, cycle, month, orbit, rotate, spin.*

Moon quiz (page 53) reinforces the children's learning that the Moon takes approximately 28 days to orbit the Earth and that the different appearance of the Moon over 28 days provides evidence for a 28-day cycle. The children could also contribute to a fact-file or database about the Moon.

Resources: information books and CD-ROMs about the Moon • a computer • planetarium websites

> **Vocabulary:** *calendar, cycle, lunar, Moon, orbit, rotate, spin.*

Changing sounds

The activities in this section develop the children's knowledge and understanding about how sounds are produced, how sounds travel, about the materials that inhibit the vibrations of sounds and about pitch and volume. The activities build on **Sound and hearing** from **Year 1**.

Feel that sound (page 54) helps the children to learn that sounds are made when objects or materials vibrate. They are asked to make careful observations and to draw conclusions about sounds from the observations. They should first have had the opportunity to explore the ways in which simple musical instruments produce sounds: encourage them to notice what they have to do to make a sound with the instrument. Children who play instruments such as the piano might have experienced the use of tuning forks and could talk about what they are for and how they are used. To strike a tuning fork without damaging it, hold it by the handle and strike the side of one of the prongs on a thick book.

Resources: cymbals and beaters • drums and drumsticks • rice • tuning forks • small bowls of water • metal bars and beaters • string • rulers • G-clamps • table-tennis balls • sellotape

> **Vocabulary:** *cymbal, tuning fork, vibrate, vibration.*

Into your ears (page 55) explores the ways in which vibrations from sound sources travel through different materials to the ear. The children should notice that sounds can travel through air and through solid objects such as walls and doors. (They can also travel through liquids.) The activity in which

Use the type of can opener that does not leave sharp edges on the can and tape the edges if they still feel sharp. Tell the children that loud noises can damage their hearing, so they must not blow the whistle near anyone's ears.

they blow a whistle close to the top of an open tin can show that sounds make the air vibrate and that this, in turn, make the balloon at the other end of the tin vibrate. The mirror til moves as the balloon vibrates and its vibrations can be seer when the reflection from the torchlight moves. We hear sound because the vibrating air makes the ear drums vibrate against small bones inside the ear.

Resources: tin can with both ends removed • balloon • loud whistle • torch • sticky tape • elastic bands

> **Vocabulary:** *vibrate, vibration.*

In **Travelling sounds** (page 56) the children learn that sound travel better through solid materials than through gases such a air. Various sound effects can be made using the 'sound effec machine', and all of them can be heard very clearly when the matchbox is held to the ear, acting in the same way as the bo structure of musical instruments such as violins and guitars. The children could tell stories using sound effects such as an old fashioned telephone dialling, screeching brakes, knocking on a door, scraping boots, plucking strings, a ticking clock and so on

Resources: matchboxes • button thread • buttons • cotton reels • small pieces of cotton cloth • spent matches

> **Vocabulary:** *air, gas, solid, sound effect, vibrate, vibration.*

Soundproofers: 1 and **2** (pages 57–58) develop the children' knowledge and understanding about materials that are effective in preventing vibrations from sound sources reaching the ear. They are asked to use a prediction to help them to decide what evidence to collect, to devise a fair comparison o materials and to carry out and evaluate their investigation Instead of testing floor-coverings, they could test materials fo soundproofing walls by placing an object that makes a continuous sound, such as a travel alarm clock or a radio, inside a box, and wrapping the box in the same amount of differen materials. They could measure how near they have to be to the box to hear the sound; or they could make ear-muffs from different materials and test their effectiveness in a similar way. Introduce *volume* for loudness. Make the most of the mathematical opportunities in these activities: measuring and recording length and handling and interpreting data.

Resources: materials to test, such as carpet, ceramic tiles, vinyl tiles, cushioned vinyl flooring, a concrete floor (or they could compare hollow and solid wooden floors)
• a metre ruler or long tape measure, or a sound sensor linked to a computer

Vocabulary: *loudness, soundproof, volume.*

High and low (page 59) develops the children's knowledge and understanding of *pitch* to describe how high or low a sound is. They learn that high or low sounds can be loud or quiet and about the effects of the size of an object on its pitch. You could also show the children how adjusting the stretch and tautness of the skin of a drum and of violin and guitar strings affects their pitch; let them compare the sounds made by thick, thin, short and long strings. They should notice that small objects tend to make higher sounds than large ones; this is because the sound waves are shorter. This could be linked with work in music: thinking about pitch.

Resources: earthenware plant pots in different sizes
• dowel or brush handle • string • elastic bands
• rulers of different lengths • metal bars or pipes of different lengths

Vocabulary: *high, loudness, low, pitch, volume.*

Pitch change (page 60) helps the children to learn that sounds can be made by air vibrating. They are asked to suggest how to alter the The children should not pick up the bottles. pitch of a sound and to test the prediction, and to describe how pitch can be altered. The more water the bottle contains, the lower the pitch of the sound it produces when tapped (because a larger volume of water is vibrating). The opposite effect is achieved when the children blow across the top of the bottle: the more water in the bottle, the *higher* the pitch of the sound. This is because the column of air vibrates: the more water there is in the bottle the less air.

Resources: glass bottles • metal tappers • water • funnel

Vocabulary: *high, low, pitch, vibrate, volume.*

Enquiry in environmental and technological contexts

The four activities in this section develop the children's skills in investigative work. They learn to plan a suitable approach for finding the answer to a question through investigation, collect and record evidence appropriately, explain the results using scientific knowledge and understanding and evaluate the evidence collected and consider its limitations.

Down to earth: 1 (page 61) encourages the children to ask scientific questions; to plan how to answer questions; to decide what kind of evidence to collect and record. They could compare patches of cleared earth about 60 cm square. Encourage them to clear patches in different types of area:

under bushes, on a lawn, in a flowerbed, by a path, on different sides of a wall, in shady and sunny places, in sheltered and exposed places and so on. When comparing patches of earth, take the opportunity for Work in dog- and cat-free areas. The children should not touch their faces while working with soil and they should wash their hands afterwards. some work on literacy: using comparatives such as *more, fewer, smaller, bigger, greater.*

Resources: small spades or trowels

Vocabulary: *clear, earth.*

Down to earth: 2 (page 62) encourages the children to collect and record data appropriately. The children could also draw plans of the cleared patches of earth and mark on them the seedlings that appear each week (using a different coloured pen each week). Do not ask them to try to identify the plants; this is very difficult from seedlings, even for familiar plants.

Resources: small wooden stakes • string • scissors

Vocabulary: *section, seedling.*

Down to earth: 3 (page 63) encourages the children to identify and describe patterns in data and to look critically at the data collected. Some patterns might emerge: for example, patches of earth underneath bushes develop few plants from seedlings, as do patches on the north side of walls. This could be because of the lack of light. Also there are usually several seedlings of the same species as the plants around them (probably because some of their seeds landed nearby). Ask the children how they think seeds from plants that cannot be seen nearby might have got there. (Remind them about seed dispersal.) Discuss any trends the children have noticed: for example, that grass tends to grow on *any* patches of bare earth or that patches of earth near to a sycamore tree have sycamore seedlings growing in them. Encourage the children to evaluate the evidence they have collected. Is there enough evidence to support any conclusions, or do they need to collect more?

Vocabulary: *dispersal, disperse, pattern, sample, seedling, summary, trend.*

In **Down to earth: 4** (page 64) the children are asked to explain the results of their investigations using their scientific knowledge and understanding. Link this with literacy work on explanations. The children are also encouraged to develop an awareness of the limitations of the evidence they have collected. Ask them to suggest reasons why any patterns have emerged: for example, grass seedlings grow on most patches of bare earth. Is this because there is a lot of grass near the patches, because grass is a very common plant or because grass can tolerate a variety of conditions? Do patches of earth in sunny places have more seedlings growing on them than those in shaded places?

Vocabulary: *conclusion, evaluate, evaluation, evidence, explanation, pattern, trend.*

The food folk

Understand that to stay healthy we need an adequate and varied diet

Are the food folk right? Yes or No

- **Explain your answers.**

Eat some fruit every day.

Miss Pear

_____

Eat some fat. It keeps you warm.

Marge

_____

Everyone needs fish once a week.

Fishy

_____

Eat some meat every day.

Lambchop

_____

Drink a lot of water.

Droplet

_____

Now try this!

- **Add another character to the food folk.**

Teachers' note Use this page to introduce the topic of healthy eating. Encourage the children to write what they know about food and health. Point out that different people have different diets and that there are many types of healthy diet, although there are certain types of food that our bodies need in order to stay healthy.

Developing Science
Year 5
© **A & C BLACK**

Scurvy at sea

Understand how a scientific idea can be tested

Scurvy is a disease that affects the skin, gums and other parts of the body. It can kill.

Scurvy used to be common among sailors – but usually only when they were at sea.

We do not know what causes scurvy. Let's list all the differences between life on sea and on land. Then we can look for the cause of the disease.

Differences

Life at home	Life at sea

What do you think caused scurvy? _____

_____

Why? _____

_____

Now try this!

- **Use books, CD-ROMs and the Internet to find out more about scurvy.**
- **Make notes:**

Cause	How doctors treated it	Which treatments worked	How to prevent scurvy

Teachers' note Tell the children that scurvy was a big problem for sailors in the fifteenth century, during the age of sea exploration, when ships were sailing on long voyages. Tell them about the symptoms of the disease (see page 5) and point out that doctors at the time did not know what caused it, but were beginning to find cures. Ask the children to list all the ideas about the cause of scurvy that might have occurred to doctors at the time.

Developing Science
Year 5
© A & C BLACK

Foods are good for you in different ways.

cauliflower · carrots · chips · pasta · orange juice · milk · chicken · lamb chop · butter · rice · bread · pineapple · tuna · biscuits · egg · naan · grapes · steak · chocolate · peanuts · sugar · cheese · cake

- ## List the foods in the correct boxes.

Foods to help you to grow	Foods for energy
_____ _____	_____ _____
_____ _____	_____ _____
_____ _____	_____ _____
_____ _____	_____ _____
Fatty foods	**Foods to keep you healthy**
_____ _____	_____ _____
_____ _____	_____ _____
_____ _____	_____ _____

Now try this!

- ## List the foods that belong in more than one group.
- ## Give reasons.

Teachers' note Provide a collection of food information leaflets from supermarkets, grocers, greengrocers, pharmacies, doctors' surgeries and websites to help the children to identify foods rich in fats or oils (for keeping warm, as stored energy), starchy/sugary foods (for energy), protein foods (for growth and repair) and foods rich in vitamins and minerals (for healthy bodies).

Developing Science
Year 5
© **A & C BLACK**

Fit for life

Recognise that we need exercise to stay healthy

Which parts of their bodies are these children exercising?

Parts of the body being exercised ✔				
arms	legs	back	heart	lungs
a				
b				
c				
d				
e				
f				
g				
h				
i				

Now try this!

- **Make notes about how different kinds of exercise affect the body.**

Teachers' note After a PE lesson, discuss the effects of exercise on the children. They could also talk about the effects (both immediate and a day later) of other types of exercise they take. In which parts of their bodies can they feel the effects of different types of exercise? Draw attention to the muscles, heart and lungs.

Developing Science
Year 5
© A & C BLACK

Feel the beat

Measure pulse rate and relate it to heart beat

• **Feel your** pulse **in these places:**

(a) (b) (c) (d)

You need

a stopwatch

In which place can you feel your pulse most easily? ☐

⚠ **Don't press on the pulse spots.**

• **Ask a friend to time 30 seconds while you count the pulse beats in your neck.**

• **Record your result on the chart.**

Place	Pulse beats in 30 seconds		
	1st try	2nd try	3rd try
neck			
inside elbow			
back of knee			
wrist			

Count twice more to check if you were right.

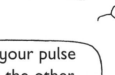

Record your pulse beats in the other places on your body.

What do you notice? _____

Now try this!

• **Find a way to count your heart beats in 30 seconds.**

• **Record your results.**

What do you notice about heart and pulse beats?

Teachers' note Revise the children's previous learning about the pulse. Ask them where they can feel their pulse (see above). If children find it difficult to find the pulse behind their knee, suggest they work in pairs, with one feeling the pulse and counting and the other timing 30 seconds. The children should rest the fingers lightly on the pulse spots. After they have completed the activity, help them to make links between the pulse and the heart beat (see page 6).

Developing Science Year 5
© A & C BLACK

Pulse change

- **Record your** pulse rate **at rest.**

  ☐ **beats in 30 seconds**

  What kind of exercise do you think will raise your pulse rate most?

  _____

You need

a stopwatch

- **Record your pulse rate after doing each exercise for two minutes.**

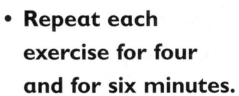

Rest for two minutes between each exercise.

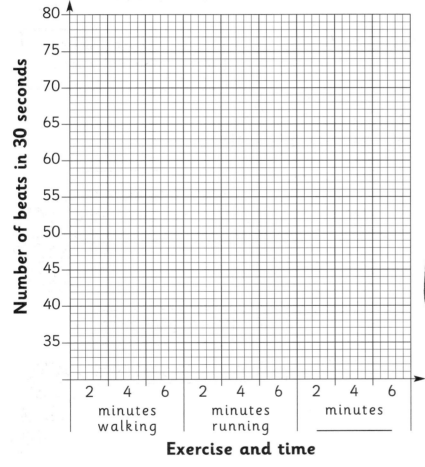

Number of beats in 30 seconds

80, 75, 70, 65, 60, 55, 50, 45, 40, 35

2 4 6   2 4 6   2 4 6

minutes walking   minutes running   minutes _____

Exercise and time

- **Repeat each exercise for four and for six minutes.**

Choose another exercise to try. Write it here.

Which exercise raised your pulse rate the most? _____

Why? _____

Now try this!

- **Check your results.**
- **Try doing each exercise after a longer rest.**

Teachers' note The children should first have completed page 18. Ask them if they think different exercises will affect pulse rate differently and if the time spent exercising will make a difference. After the activity, remind the children that where they can feel their pulse they are feeling the effects of their heart beat.

Developing Science
Year 5
© A & C BLACK

Drug watch

Understand that tobacco, alcohol and other drugs can be harmful

Which of these drugs can help or harm your body or mind? How?

- Write what you know. Note any questions you have. Find the answers.

Use books and the Internet.

Drug	The good it can do	The harm it can do	My questions
alcohol			
aspirin			
heroin			
tobacco			

Now try this!

- Choose another drug to research.
- Find out why people take it and how it affects them. Make notes.

Teachers' note Explain that a drug is a substance that has an effect on people's minds or bodies and ask the children to name any they know about. Why do people take drugs? Point out that people take some drugs as medicines to help them to get over an illness or to prevent health problems and that some people take drugs because they enjoy their effects, but that all drugs can be harmful if used wrongly (see page 6).

Developing Science
Year 5
© **A & C BLACK**

Travelling seeds: 1

Understand that seeds can be dispersed in many ways

- **Examine some seeds from different plants.**
- **Draw and label the seeds.**

  How do you think the seeds are $\boxed{\text{dispersed}}$ **?**
- **Give reasons.**

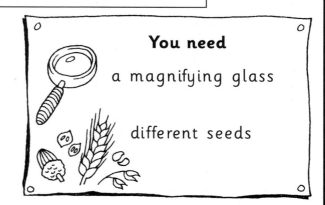

You need

a magnifying glass

different seeds

Seed	How I think it is dispersed	Why I think this

Now try this!

- **Use information books to check your answers.**

Teachers' note Explain that *dispersal* means the scattering of seeds by a plant, and that plants have different ways of doing this. Show them seeds that are dispersed in different ways (by the wind, animals, explosion or water): for example, ash, coconut, dandelion, grasses, rowan, sycamore, teasel, thistle. Ask the children to say how they think they are dispersed. Continued on page 22.

Travelling seeds: 2

Understand that seeds can be dispersed in many ways

How are these seeds dispersed?

- ## Cut out the pictures and sort them into sets:

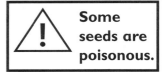

⚠ Some seeds are poisonous.

Dispersed by wind	Dispersed by animals	Dispersed by explosion	Dispersed by water

apple · ash · beech · burdock

cedar · cherry · coconut · columbine

cotoneaster · couch grass · fig · fir

  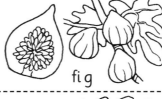 

laburnum · lupin · oak · poppy

redcurrant · rowan · Scots pine · sea rocket

strawberry · sycamore · teasel · thistle

 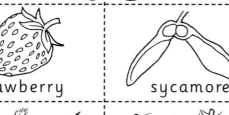    

timothy grass · willow · yellow iris · yew

Teachers' note Use this with page 21. Encourage the children to look carefully at the pictures and to identify features discussed in the previous activity that make the seeds suitable for dispersal in different ways.

**Developing Science
Year 5**
© A & C BLACK

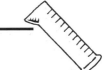

Wake up seeds!

Recognise the conditions seeds need in order to germinate

- **Read the fact-file.**

  What conditions do you think seeds need in order to | germinate |**?**

  _____

  _____

- **Plan an investigation to find out if you are right.**

What I shall do:

Change one thing at a time.

I shall need:

What I shall observe or measure:

What I expect to happen if I am right:

Teachers' note Explain that the germination of a seed means the sprouting of a root and a shoot and is not the same as the growth of the plant; growth follows germination. After the children have listed the conditions they think affect germination, encourage them to think how to test one condition at a time.

Developing Science
Year 5
© A & C BLACK

23

Flower power

Understand that insects pollinate some flowers

How are some plants pollinated?

- **Write in the speech bubbles to explain what happens during** pollination.

stigma (female part of flower)

pollen on stamen (male part of flower)

ovules in ovary

petal

- **Find out how the shapes and colours of flowers can help in pollination.**

Teachers' note Revise what the children have learned about dispersal and germination. Discuss where on a plant the seeds can be found, and at what point in the development of the flower. Point out that seeds do not appear automatically when a flower dies, that plants have male and female parts, each of which produces an essential ingredient: these combine to create seeds and this is called fertilisation.

Developing Science
Year 5
© **A & C BLACK**

All about plants

Learn about the life cycles of flowering plants

- **Write the definitions for this plant glossary.**

Use information books.

disperse	
dormant	
fertilise	
germinate	
ovary	
ovule	
petal	
pollen	
pollinate	
seed	
stamen	
stigma	

- **Find other words that describe parts of plants and what plants do.**
- **Write definitions.**

Teachers' note It would be helpful if the children have completed pages 21–24, as the words on this page should have been introduced during those activities. Encourage the children to discuss the meaning of each word, to revise their previous work in which the word was used and to check it in a comprehensive dictionary or encyclopedia.

Developing Science
Year 5
© A & C BLACK

Learn about the life cycles of flowering plants

• **Write a heading and caption for each stage in the life cycle of the poppy.**

Word-bank

bud   pollination
dispersal   seed
fertilisation seedling
flower   seed pod
      germination

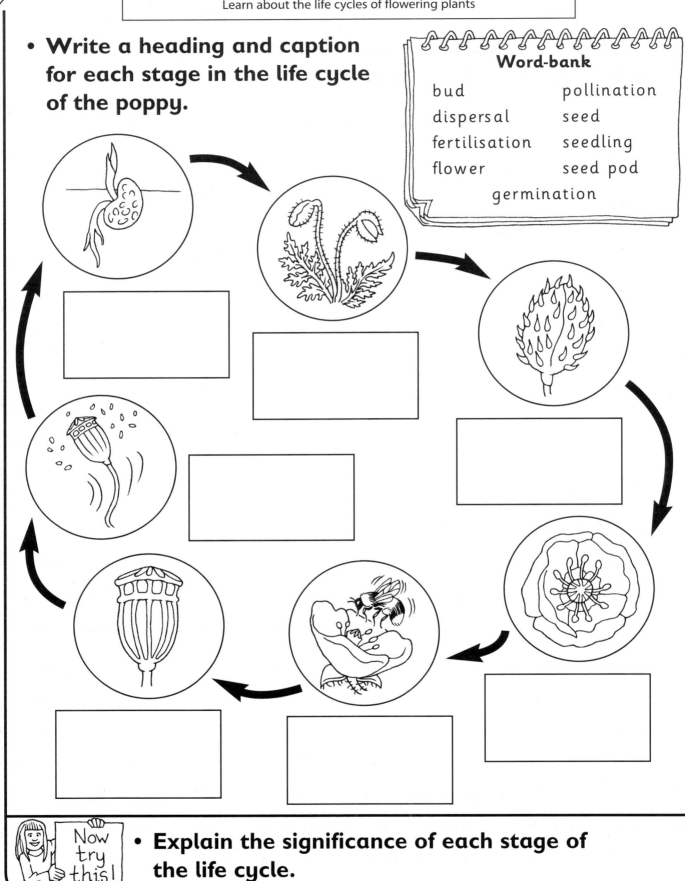

• **Explain the significance of each stage of the life cycle.**

Now try this!

Teachers' note The children should first have completed pages 21–25. They could start on this life cycle at any point but it makes sense to begin with the top left-hand picture (germination). Discuss how the poppy is similar to other flowering plants. For the extension activity, ask the children to think about what each stage of the life cycle is for and what would happen (or not happen) if that stage did not occur.

Developing Science
Year 5
© A & C BLACK

The cycle of life

Understand that adults have young and that these grow into adults

- **On the timeline, mark and label where you think the following stages of life begin and end:**

| babyhood | childhood | adolescence |

| adulthood | old age |

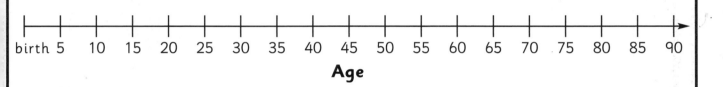

birth 5 10 15 20 25 30 35 40 45 50 55 60 65 70 75 80 85 90

Age

- **Explain your answers.**

_____

_____

_____

_____

_____

Now try this!

- **Find out what is meant by** gestation.
- **Make notes about the gestation times of humans and other mammals.**

Teachers' note Tell the children that they are going to consider the life of humans, and ask them to suggest the stages into which a human life could be divided. Introduce the terms *babyhood, childhood, adolescence, adulthood* and *old age*, and discuss what they mean. Ask the children to discuss in their groups when they think these stages begin and end.

Developing Science
Year 5
© A & C BLACK

Solid, liquid or gas?

Recognise differences between solids, liquids and gases

- **List some of the solids, liquids and gases in the picture.**

Solids	Liquids	Gases

- **Write some characteristics of:**

solids

_____

_____

_____

liquids

_____

_____

_____

gases

_____

_____

_____

- **Name and describe another solid, another liquid and another gas.**

Teachers' note Begin by identifying solid materials in the classroom, any liquids and a gas (air). Ask the children how they know when something is solid. How are liquids different from solids? How are gases different from solids? How are gases different from liquids? Show the children a collection of containers (bags, baskets, boxes and airtight jars or bottles) and ask them if they could keep a solid, a liquid or a gas in them.

Developing Science
Year 5
© A & C BLACK

As heavy as air

Understand that air has weight and is all around us

Do you think objects become lighter or heavier or stay the same if you fill them with air? Why?

_____

_____

_____

• **Try this:**

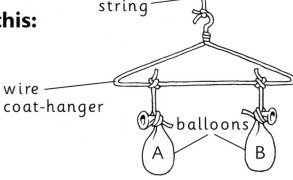

string

wire coat-hanger

balloons

A   B

⚠ Do not inflate balloons by mouth.

Are the balloons balanced? _____

• **Try inflating one balloon and then both balloons.**

• **Count how many 'pumps' of air you put in.**

Amount of air		Are the balloons balanced? If not, which one is lighter?
Balloon A	Balloon B	
0 pumps	0 pumps	
1 pump	0 pumps	
0 pumps	1 pump	
3 pumps	0 pumps	
0 pumps	3 pumps	
1 pump	6 pumps	

Now try this!

• **Explain your results.**

Teachers' note After the children have named and discussed objects containing air (see page 8), ask them if a balloon is heavier empty or when it contains air, and why. Ensure that they understand that if two objects are hung from a balanced bar (or coat-hanger) they will be level if they are the same weight but that if one is heavier that side of the balance will be lower.

Developing Science
Year 5
© A & C BLACK

Air holes

Recognise that sponges are solid materials with air in the 'gaps'

- **Put each object on the list into a bowl of water.**
- **Squeeze the object if you can.**
- **Record your observations.**

You need

a bowl of water

the objects on the list below

List of objects

ball

balloon (inflated but not tied)

beach ball (inflated, but take out the stopper)

drinks can

plastic bottles (no tops)

small pottery vase or jug

sponge

Object	What happened	What made this happen

Now try this!

- **Find out what happens when you pour water into:**
  - **a jar of marbles**
  - **a jar of sand**
  - **a jar of nuts and bolts**
  - **a jar of gravel.**

Teachers' note Show the children an empty bottle and ask them what it contains. Point out that most 'empty' things contain air, unless the air has been sucked out of them (even an uninflated balloon has some air in it). Tell them that the activities they are going to try will show them that empty containers have air inside them.

Developing Science
Year 5
© A & C BLACK

30

Soaking in

Understand that soils have air trapped within them

Examine the soils using a magnifying glass.

Which soil do you think contains the most air?

Why? _____

_____

You need

4 different types of soil, labelled A, B, C, D

4 clear plastic pots

a magnifying glass

a measuring cylinder

You can measure the amount of air in soil:

1 Measure the same amount of each soil into a plastic pot.

A   B   C   D

2 Fill a measuring cylinder with water.

3 Slowly pour water onto each soil until it stops soaking in.

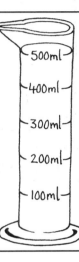

4 How much water soaked into the soil?

Soil sample	Volume of water in measuring cylinder		Volume of water that soaked into soil	Observations
	Before	After		
A				
B				
C				
D				

Now try this!

• **Write what your results tell you about the amount of air in each soil.**

Teachers' note The children should first have completed page 30. Ask them why it might be useful for soil to have air trapped in it, what gardeners do to aerate the soil and why they like to have worms in the garden. What do they think will happen to water poured onto soil that contains no air? What will happen if the soil contains a lot of air? Remind them what happened when they immersed containers in water.

Developing Science
Year 5
© A & C BLACK

Where does it go?

Recognise that gases are formed when liquids evaporate

> I put some water in this saucer yesterday.
> I left it overnight.
> Today there is no water left.

Ahmed

The children in Ahmed's class had different ideas about what happened to the water.

- **Write their explanations in the speech bubbles.**

Which explanation do you think is right?

How could you test it?

_____

_____

_____

> Think of a way to stop the water disappearing.

- **Plan a fair test to find out where water goes when it dries up.**

Teachers' note Before they begin this activity the children should measure some water into a saucer and leave it in the classroom overnight. The next day, ask them to observe the saucer and to check if the same amount of water is still in it. If not (as is probable), where has it gone? Write up the children's ideas.

Developing Science
Year 5
© A & C BLACK

Where does it come from?

- **Observe an empty can and describe what it looks like and feels like:**

_____

_____

_____

_____

_____

You need

an empty can with no label

ice

- **Put some ice cubes into the can.**
- **Label the picture to record what you observe.**

What can you feel on the outside of the can? _____

Is it all over the can? _____

- **Explain what you think has happened:** _____

_____

_____

_____

Now try this!

- **Find out how scientists explain what happened.**

Use information books to help you research what happened.

Teachers' note It would be helpful if the children had already completed page 32. Give the children a clean, shiny can with no label. Encourage them to express their ideas about what happens to the can. If they use the word *condensation*, ask them what condensation is – what it is made of.

Developing Science
Year 5
© A & C BLACK

Test it

Plan a fair test to evaluate explanations

- **Plan a fair test for your explanation of the water that appears on a can of ice.**

My explanation:

How I shall test my explanation:

I shall change only this:	I shall keep all these things the same:

What I shall observe:	What I expect to happen if my explanation is right:

Teachers' note The children should first have completed page 33. Encourage the children to think of a way to prove their explanation wrong (this is easier than trying to prove it is right) or to try to stop the condensation happening ('If your explanation is right, what will happen if …').

Developing Science
Year 5
© A & C BLACK

What do you know?

Review understanding of solids, liquids and gases

What do you know about solids, liquids and gases and the ways in which they change?

- **Draw lines and write sentences to link the words in the shapes.**

Word-bank

change	melt
cool	pour
evaporate	shape
flow	volume
freeze	warm

liquid

solid

Water is a liquid.

water

powder

steam

ice

gas

You have made a concept map.

Now try this!

- **Add three new words to your concept map.**
- **Link these new words to as many of the others as you can.**

Teachers' note Copy this page onto A3 paper. If necessary, explain to the children that a concept map helps them to review what they understand about a topic. They could complete another concept map at the end of the topic to assess what they have learned.

Developing Science
Year 5
© A & C BLACK

Water, water everywhere

Understand that evaporation is when a liquid turns to a gas

- **Find out what is the best puddle-drying weather.**

You need

chalk

string

a ruler

a 2-litre measuring jug

① Make a puddle of the same size in the same place each day.

② Every half hour, chalk a line round the edge of the puddle.

③ Cut a piece of string the same length as the chalk line.

④ Measure the string.

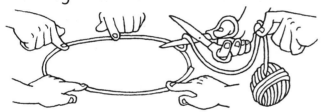

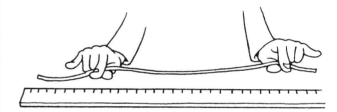

- **Record your results.**

Date	Weather	Distance round edge of puddle				
		Start	½ hour	1 hour	1½ hours	2 hours

Now try this!

- **Write an explanation of your results.**

Teachers' note Encourage the children to observe how quickly puddles in the playground dry up on different days. What do they think affects the time it takes for the puddles to dry? They should record the weather conditions on each day that they take their measurements: windy, sunny, wet, dry, calm, foggy, raining and so on.

Developing Science
Year 5
© **A & C BLACK**

Drying up

Does the shape of the container make any difference to how quickly water evaporates**?**

- **Plan an investigation to find out.**

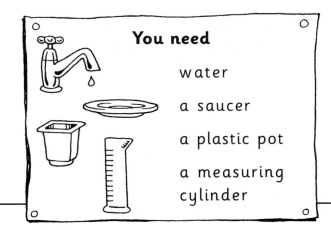

You need

water

a saucer

a plastic pot

a measuring cylinder

What I shall do:

How I shall make the test fair:	How often I shall observe the water:	What I think will happen and why:

Results:

Make a chart.

Now try this!

- **Explain your results and your conclusions to a partner.**

Teachers' note Ask the children why the shape of a container might affect evaporation speed (in a wide container a greater surface area of water is exposed to air, allowing faster evaporation). Revise the idea that the same volume of water can appear greater or smaller, depending on the container. The children should use the same volume of water in each container.

Developing Science
Year 5
© A & C BLACK

Washday: 1

Explain everyday examples of 'drying' in scientific terms

What do people you know think is the quickest way to dry their washing?

- **Do a survey.**

Method	Number of people		Advantages	Disadvantages
	Tally	Total		
outdoor line				
indoor folding airer				
indoor clothes-horse				
outdoor rotary line				
tumble dryer				

- **Make a list of the important factors in drying things.**

Teachers' note The children could conduct their survey partly for homework (questioning friends and members of their family) and partly at school (questioning people who work in or visit the school). Continued on page 39.

**Developing Science
Year 5
© A & C BLACK**

Washday: 2

Construct a fair test

What is the quickest way to dry the washing?

On an outdoor clothes line.

Andy

On an indoor clothes line.

Jade

In an airtight box.

Mina

In a tumble dryer.

Liam

Whose washing will dry first? _____

Why? _____

_____

How will the children know whose washing dries first?

_____

_____

How can they make their test fair?

_____

_____

_____

_____

_____

- **Plan a fair test on different ways of drying pieces of sugar paper.**

You can see when sugar paper is dry.

Teachers' note Use this with page 38. Discuss what happens when materials dry (they lose water) and ask the children where the water goes and what makes it evaporate quickly. Help them to identify factors that make the test fair: the size of the item, the amount of water it has absorbed, the type of material.

Developing Science
Year 5
© A & C BLACK

Into the air

Do all liquids evaporate?

- **Plan a fair test to find out which of the liquids on the list evaporates most quickly.**

Liquids

aftershave

cooking oil

lemonade

perfume

washing-up liquid

My prediction:

What I shall do:

What I need:

What I shall keep the same:

What I shall change:

What I shall observe or measure:

How I shall record my observations and measurements:

How I shall know if my prediction was right:

Teachers' note It would be helpful if the children had already completed pages 36–39. Ask them how they will know if a liquid has evaporated. Discuss their predictions and encourage them to measure the same amount of each liquid into the same types of container and to put them all in the same place. Point out that all the liquids will evaporate eventually.

Developing Science
Year 5
© A & C BLACK

What a pong!

- **Predict: Will you be able to smell perfume more strongly if it is:**

You need

some cheap perfume

a small dish

a long tape measure

in an open bottle?   in a small dish?   on someone's skin?

- **Use the same number of squirts of perfume each time.**

- **Start about 10 metres from the perfume.**

- **Walk towards it until you can smell it.**

- **Measure the distance at which you can smell it:**

sniff

10 metres

Repeat the test with different people.

- **Record your results.**

Where the perfume was	Smelling distance (metres)			
	1st try	2nd try	3rd try	4th try
in an open bottle				
in a small dish				
on the skin				

What did you find out? _____

_____

Now try this!

- **Write an explanation of your results.**

Teachers' note It would be helpful if the children had already completed page 40. It is important that those children involved in the test begin at a distance from which they cannot smell the perfume; they should gradually move closer to it until they can. They should record the distance at which they first smelled it. The words '1st try', '2nd try', and so on, could be masked and replaced with the names of the children in the group.

Developing Science
Year 5
© A & C BLACK

The strongest pong

- **Find a way to test which is the strongest smelling perfume.**

  My prediction:

  _____

  will be the strongest smelling perfume because _____

  _____

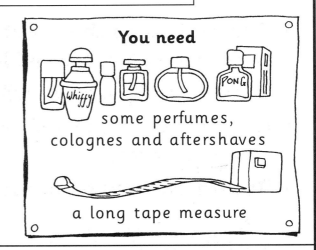

You need

some perfumes, colognes and aftershaves

a long tape measure

This is what I shall do:

To make the test fair I shall keep these the same:	I shall change only this:

I shall measure and observe this:

I shall record my results like this:

Now try this!

How will you know which is the strongest smelling perfume?

Teachers' note The children should first have completed page 41. For a fair test, the children should use the same amount of each perfume, in the same type of container (or placed on the skin in a similar place on people; the only thing they change is the perfume used). The strongest will be smelled from the greatest distance.

Developing Science
Year 5
© A & C BLACK

On the boil

Understand that the boiling point of water is 100°C

- **Draw a line on the graph to predict what will happen to water when it is heated for ten minutes.**

  At what temperature will the water boil? [ ] **°C**

- **Observe what happens when the water is heated.**

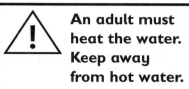

An adult must heat the water. Keep away from hot water.

- **Record the results on the graph.**

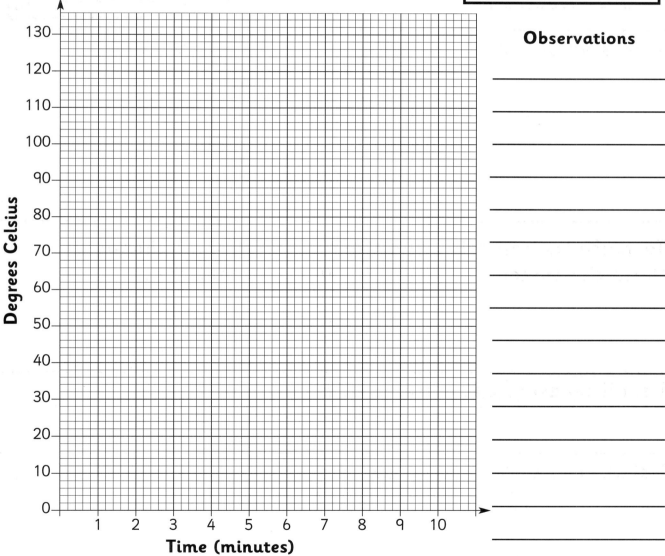

Observations

_____

_____

_____

_____

_____

_____

_____

_____

_____

_____

_____

_____

_____

- **Write what you have learned about the behaviour of water when it is heated.**

Teachers' note The children should draw a line to indicate what they predict will happen to the temperature of the water over the course of ten minutes. To record the actual temperature during the investigation, they should draw crosses on the graph in another colour and then join the crosses with a line. This can then be compared with their prediction.

Developing Science
Year 5
© A & C BLACK

Round and round

Understand that water evaporates from oceans, seas and lakes, condenses as clouds and falls as rain

- **Continue the questions and answers until you get back to the start.**
- **Write questions that begin 'Where...'**

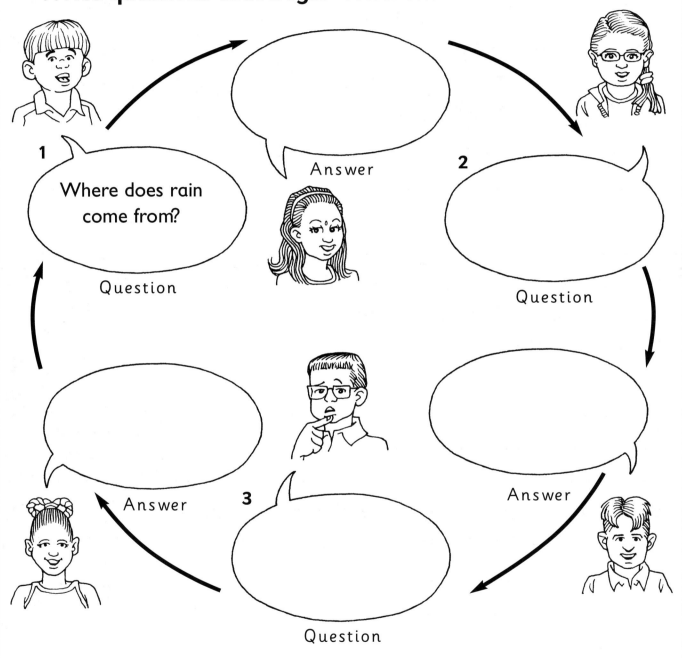

1 Question

Where does rain come from?

Answer

2 Question

Answer

3 Question

Answer

- **Write an explanation for each answer.**

Now try this!

Use the words 'condense' and 'evaporate'.

Teachers' note Review the children's understanding of evaporation and condensation. Model how to complete the activity sheet by reading the question with the children and asking them to think of an answer. If they answer 'The sky' ask them where in the sky the rain comes from and if it rains when the sky is clear and blue. Help them to think of the next 'Where' question ('Where do the clouds come from?').

**Developing Science
Year 5**
© A & C BLACK

Flat Earth

Hundreds of years ago people thought that the Earth was shaped like a flat disc:

> I see no land. The edge of the Earth must be yonder.

> Go no further. The edge cannot be far away.

What do you think made people think this?

_____

_____

What everyday observations might have helped scientists to show that the Earth is roughly a sphere?

_____

_____

_____

> Think about horizons and the Sun and Moon.

> Think about sea voyages.

What might have made it difficult for people to believe that the Earth is roughly a sphere?

_____

_____

_____

> Try standing up model people in different places on a ball.

Now try this!

How do we know that the Earth is spherical?

• List the ways in which you can check this fact.

Teachers' note Ask the children what they know about the shape of the Earth, and how they know. How can the facts be checked? Point out that, although the children cannot carry out experiments to check the facts, they can be checked in secondary sources.

**Developing Science
Year 5
© A & C BLACK**

45

Heavenly spheres

Recognise that the Earth, the Sun and the Moon are approximately spherical

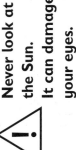

⚠ ! **Never look at the Sun. It can damage your eyes.**

- **Write down any questions you have about the shapes and sizes of the Earth, Sun and Moon.**
- **Where do you think you can find the answers?   Which questions can you answer?**

My questions	Where I can find the answer			The answers I found
	Observations I can make	Books and CD-ROMs	Websites	

Now try this!

- **Write a report about the shapes and sizes of the Earth, Sun and Moon.**

Teachers' note It would be helpful if the children had already completed page 45. Ask them what they know about the shape of the Sun and Moon and why it is easier to find out about their shapes by observation than it is to find out about the shape of the Earth. Can they put the Earth, Sun and Moon in order of size?

Developing Science
Year 5
© A & C BLACK

Moving Sun

Understand that the Sun appears to move across the sky during the day

- **Draw the shadows of the school and the trees at different times of the day.**

Notice where the Sun is in each picture.

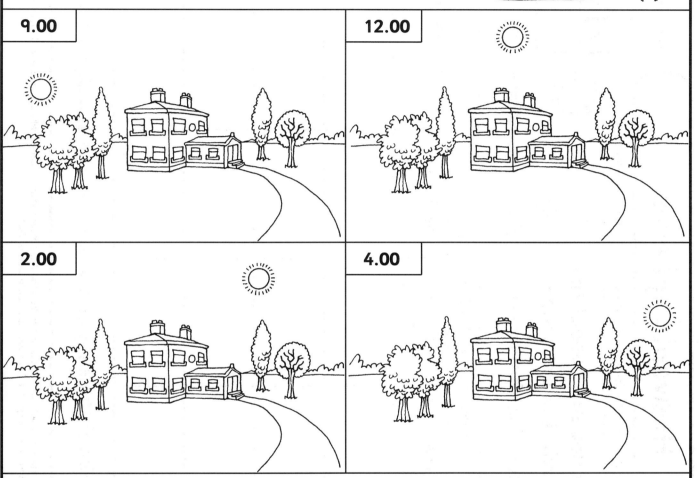

9.00

12.00

2.00

4.00

- **Draw a picture of your school, seen from the north, showing the whole building.**
- **Make four copies of the picture.**
- **Record the position of the Sun at different times.**

⚠ **Never look at the Sun. It can damage your eyes.**

Now try this!

- **Explain why you see the Sun in different places.**
- **Describe how the shadows change and what makes them change.**

Teachers' note Discuss the pictures with the children and remind them of their work on shadows in Year 3. It might be necessary to set up a shadow stick to remind them about the changes in the length and direction of the shadow.

**Developing Science
Year 5**
© A & C BLACK

Fun in the sun

Make an Egyptian sundial.

- **Cut open a cereal box like this:**

Cut off this side

Cut off this end

⚠ **Never look at the Sun.**

- **Put the box on level ground facing the Sun.**

- **Draw a line at the end of the shadow.**
- **Write the time.**

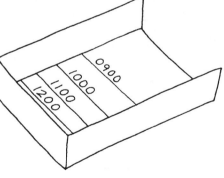

0900
1000
1100
1200

- **Repeat this every hour.**

  Your sundial should look like this by the end of the morning:

  What do you notice about the lines for the afternoon times? _____

  _____

  _____

Now try this!

- **Explain your observations about the markings of the hours on your sundial.**

  Did the box face in the same direction for each hour?
- **Explain the reason for this.**

Teachers' note It would be helpful if the children had already completed page 47. They should cut the front or back and one end off a cereal box. Encourage them to notice in which direction they must point the intact end of the cereal box each hour in order for it to face the Sun, and discuss why this direction changes.

**Developing Science
Year 5**
© A & C BLACK

Rise and shine

Understand that the Sun rises in the East and sets in the West

- **Make a line graph to show the times of sunrise and sunset on the first day of each month.**
- **Mark the times with a cross.**
- **Join the crosses with a line.**

Use a diary, newspapers or the Internet.

Key

sunrise yellow

sunset ✗✗✗ red

What patterns do you notice in the times of sunrise and sunset?

_____

_____

_____

_____

_____

_____

_____

_____

_____

_____

_____

_____

_____

_____

Time (y-axis: 03.00, 04.00, 05.00, 06.00, 07.00, 08.00, 09.00, 10.00, 11.00, 12.00, 13.00, 14.00, 15.00, 16.00, 17.00, 18.00, 19.00, 20.00, 21.00, 22.00, 23.00)

Date

Teachers' note Introduce the activity by asking the children if they know what *lighting-up time* means. You can point this out in newspapers for different days in the same week (it is usually found near the weather forecast). Ask the children why the time at which drivers have to switch on their headlights is not the same every day.

A year under the Sun

Understand that the Earth takes a year to make one complete orbit of the Sun

What do you know about the link between the Sun and a year?

• **Find out more.**

Write notes.

What I know:

My questions:

The answers:

• **Use your notes to help you write a report about how the Sun is important in the calendar.**

Teachers' note Introduce the activity by asking the children what they know about the meaning of *year*. Write up their responses and ask them what they think the connection is between the Earth's movement, the Sun, the length of the year and the length of a day.

**Developing Science
Year 5**
© A & C BLACK

Moonrise

This picture was drawn by someone facing south.

The position of the Moon was marked every hour.

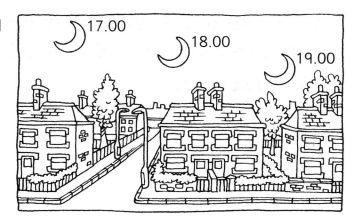

17.00 18.00 19.00

• **Draw a picture of a place near your home.**

• **Face south to look at the Moon.**

• **Every hour, draw the position of the Moon and write the time.**

⚠ An adult should help.

Now try this!

What pattern do you notice in the changing position of the Moon?

• **Write an explanation of your observations.**

Teachers' note This activity is ideal for an autumn homework. Remind the children what causes the apparent movement of the Sun across the sky. Discuss how sometimes objects appear to move in relation to others, for example: a car in which they are seated may appear to move when, in fact, an adjacent one is moving.

Developing Science
Year 5
© A & C BLACK

Moonwatch

Understand that the Moon takes about 28 days to orbit the Earth

Look at the shape of the Moon each day for four weeks.

- **Draw the Moon on the chart.**

On some days you might not be able to see the Moon.

	Monday	Tuesday	Wednesday	Thursday	Friday	Saturday	Sunday
Week 1							
Week 2							
Week 3							
Week 4							

Now try this!

- **What pattern do you notice in your observations?**
- **Write an explanation of the pattern.**

52

Teachers' note The children should first have completed page 51. This activity can be carried out in conjunction with homework in which the children record the shape of the Moon each evening in a notebook. Start the activity about three days after the New Moon, but point out that on cloudy days, and at the time of the new Moon, the Moon cannot be seen.

Developing Science
Year 5
© **A & C BLACK**

Moon quiz

- **Help the children to answer these questions.**

Use information books, CD-ROMs, videos and the Internet.

What is a lunar month?

How is a lunar month different from a calendar month?

What is the 'dark side' of the Moon?

Why can't we see the 'dark side' of the Moon?

Now try this!

- **Write another question about the Moon.**
- **Give it to a friend to answer.**

Teachers' note The children should first have completed page 51. To help them to understand the movement of the Moon around the Earth and the effects of the rotation of the Earth and Moon, you could use a model (see page 12).

Developing Science
Year 5
© A & C BLACK

Feel that sound

- **Use the objects to make a sound.**
- **Describe what you hear, see and feel.**

You need

a cymbal and beater	a G-clamp
a drum and drumstick	a ruler
a few grains of rice	string
a metal bar and beater	a table-tennis ball
a tuning fork	sellotape
a small bowl of water	

cymbal and beater

rice

drum

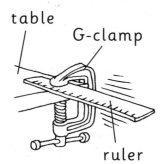

table

G-clamp

ruler

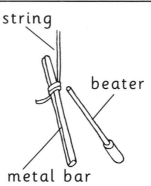

string

beater

metal bar

Now try this!

- **Strike a tuning fork.**
- **Move the tuning fork along a piece of paper.**
- **Dip the tuning fork into a bowl of water.**
- **Hold the tuning fork next to a table-tennis ball.**
- **Describe what you hear, see and feel.**

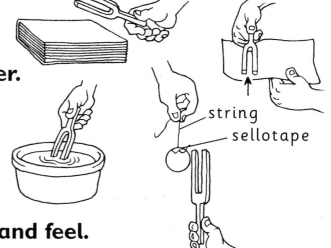

string

sellotape

Teachers' note Encourage the children to notice the movement of the objects that produce sounds, and introduce the word *vibrate*. They should notice that some objects (such as cymbals and metal bars or pipes) continue to make a sound for a few seconds because they continue to vibrate. Ask the children what happens to the sound of a vibrating metal bar or cymbal when they touch it.

Developing Science
Year 5
© **A & C BLACK**

Into your ears

- **Listen to the sounds you hear outside the classroom.**

- **List the objects and materials through which the sounds pass before they reach your ears:**

Sound	What it passes through

You need

a tin can with both ends removed

⚠ **Sharp edges should be covered with thick sticky tape.**

a balloon with the neck cut off

a loud whistle

a torch

a tiny mirror tile

sticky tape

an elastic band

⚠ **Do not blow a whistle close to anyone's ear.**

- **Set up the materials like this and blow the whistle:**

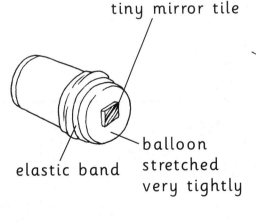

tiny mirror tile

elastic band

balloon stretched very tightly

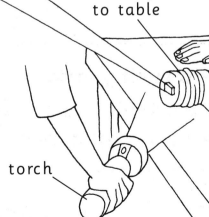

can taped to table

whistle

torch

- **Record what you see.**

Now try this!

- **Explain how the sounds get from the object that makes them to your ears.**

Teachers' note The children should first have completed page 54. Begin by asking them to sit in silence and listen to the sounds outside the classroom. Can they tell where they are coming from? Can they hear everything that happens outside the classroom? Ask them for their ideas about how the sounds reach their ears. They could make a note of their ideas to return to later, to check what they have learned.

**Developing Science
Year 5**
© A & C BLACK

Travelling sounds

Identify the types of material through which sounds travel

You need

button thread

a button

scissors

matchbox tray

a cotton reel

a small, damp handkerchief

2 spent wooden matchsticks

- **Make a sound-effects machine:**

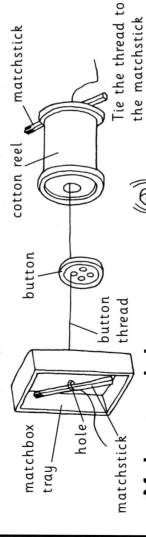

matchbox tray

hole

matchstick

button

cotton reel

button thread

matchstick

Tie the thread to the matchstick

Work with a friend who holds the matchbox tray.

... holding the matchstick and scraping the thread around the inside of the cotton reel.

- **Make sounds by:**

... moving the button backwards and forwards.

... twirling the thread like a skipping rope and then pulling it tight.

... pulling a damp cloth along the thread.

- **Repeat the sound effects while your friend holds the matchbox tray over his or her ear.**
- **Swap places and write about what you hear.**

Now try this!

Teachers' note Pierce a small hole in the tray of the matchbox and help the children to thread the button onto the thread though the matchbox, and the other through the cotton reel, and tie the ends to matchsticks to secure them. Ask them what objects and materials the sounds are travelling through when they listen to them.

Developing Science
Year 5
© A & C BLACK

Soundproofers: 1

- **Plan a fair test to find out which of these floor-coverings are the best soundproofers:**

| ceramic tiles | carpet | vinyl tiles | cushioned vinyl | concrete |

- **Your test should help you to put the materials in order:**

| quietest | ⟶ | noisiest |

I shall do this:	I need:
I shall keep these things the same:	I shall change only this:
I shall observe and measure these:	How I shall record my results:
How I shall know which is the quietest floor covering:	My prediction:

Teachers' note It would be helpful if the children had already completed page 56. Ask them to think of places and times when it is useful to stop sounds from travelling from one place to another and to describe the ways in which they have seen this carried out. What materials are used? What characteristics do these materials have? Continued on page 58.

Developing Science
Year 5
© A & C BLACK

Decide whether results support predictions

- **Use this graph to record the distances from which you could hear a coin dropping onto a floor surface.**

Work in a large space such as a hall or corridor.

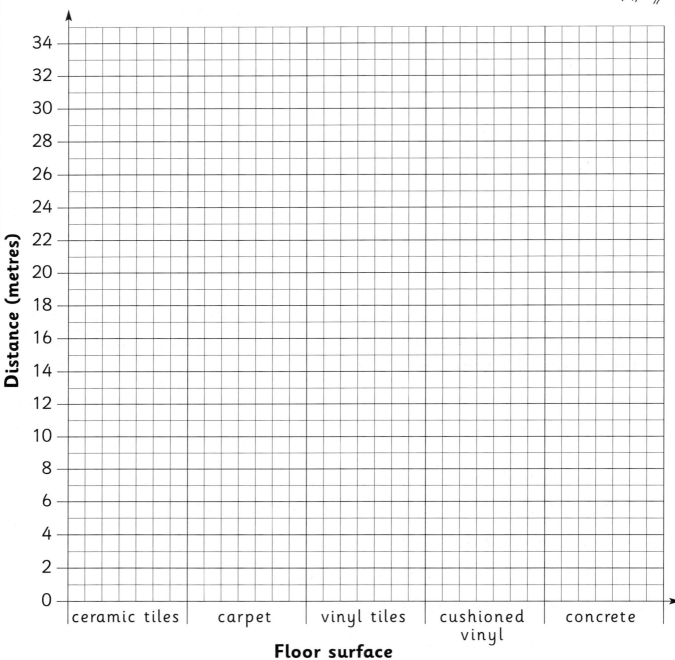

Floor surface

- **Explain why some materials are better soundproofers than others.**

Teachers' note Use this with page 57. The children could test a different collection of materials: if so, mask the words along the bottom of the graph and ask the children to write their own. There are various other ways of testing the materials (see page 12).

Developing Science
Year 5
© A & C BLACK

58

High and low

Understand that the word 'pitch' describes how high or low a sound is

- **Hang the plant pots from the dowel like this:**

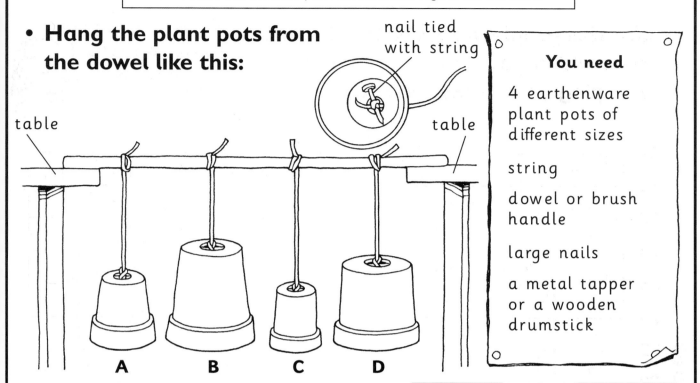

table

nail tied with string

table

You need

4 earthenware plant pots of different sizes

string

dowel or brush handle

large nails

a metal tapper or a wooden drumstick

A   B   C   D

- **Predict what your plant pots will sound like when tapped:**

lowest sound	→	highest sound

- **Find out and record your results:**

Will your results be the same if you:

- **tap metal bars or pipes of different lengths?**
- **pluck elastic bands of different sizes?**
- **twang rulers of different lengths?**
- **Predict and then find out.**
- **Record what you did and your results.**

Now try this!

- **Write what factors were important in making the sounds high-pitched or low-pitched.**

Teachers' note Play some recorded songs that are distinctly high or low: include both soprano and bass or baritone voices. Ask the children to raise their arms when they hear high-pitched singing and to lower them when they hear low-pitched singing. Re-play the music at different volumes. Point out that you have made it louder or quieter, not higher or lower.

Developing Science
Year 5
© **A & C BLACK**

Pitch change

Understand that sounds can be made by air vibrating

Will this bottle of water make a high or low sound when you tap it?

water

You need

a strong glass bottle

a metal tapper

a funnel

water

_____

- **Check your prediction.**

_____

⚠️ **An adult should place the bottle on the table.**
Do not lift it or move it.

How can you make the sound higher?

_____

How can you make the sound lower?

_____

- **Check your ideas. Be sure to tap the bottle very gently.**
- **Explain what makes a sound high or low.**

_____

Will the results be the same if you blow across the top of the bottle? _____

- **Find out and record your results.**

water

_____

Now try this!

- **Write an explanation of the results of the two investigations.**

Teachers' note It would be helpful if the children had already completed page 59. Ask them what vibrated to make the sound when they tapped the bottle. What vibrates when they blow across the top of it?

Developing Science
Year 5
© A & C BLACK

Down to earth: 1

Ask scientific questions and plan how to answer them

If you clear the grass and other plants from a patch of earth, will it stay bare? _____

- **Explain your answer:** _____

_____

Will the same happen to any patch of bare earth?

- **Make brief notes about how you could investigate this.**

How many patches of earth will you clear?

Where will you clear them?

How big should the patches be?

Will you count the total number of plants?

After how long will you count them?

Will you look for different types of plant?

- **Write two other questions about how to make the investigation fair.**
- **Make notes about how to investigate them.**
- **Choose the best question to investigate.**

Teachers' note Use this with pages 62–64. Ask the children about their observations of gardens. What happens to patches of bare earth that have been cleared of weeds? Do they stay clear? Does it make any difference where the bare earth is? How can they find out if the same always happens? Encourage them to plan an investigation that includes clearing patches of earth in different types of location (see page 13). Continued on page 62.

Developing Science
Year 5
© **A & C BLACK**

• **Count the seedlings that have grown on each patch of earth.**

If there are too many to count, you could divide the patch into sections like this:

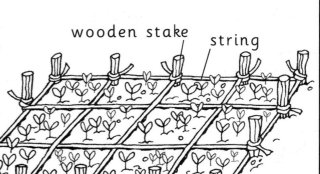

wooden stake   string

Count the seedlings in one section.

Multiply this number by the number of sections.

For example:
18 seedlings
x 12 sections
216 seedlings

• **Record the number of seedlings that have grown on each patch of bare earth.**

Location of patch of earth	Number of seedlings

Now try this!

What else can you observe, measure and record?

• **Make a chart.**

Teachers' note Use this with pages 61 and 63–64. The children should begin the investigation by clearing patches of earth in different locations. These should be left for at least a week. Some children could devise ways of collecting and recording data, but most will need help. Ask them where they think the seedlings have come from. Continued on page 63.

Developing Science
Year 5
© A & C BLACK

Down to earth: 3

Identify and describe patterns in data

• **Write a recount of what you did in your investigation.**

Heading:

My question:

What I did:	My equipment:

Summary of results:

Patterns or trends in results:

Was your sample big enough for the patterns or trends to be meaningful?

What else I need to do:

Teachers' note Use this with pages 61–62 and 64. Ask the children if they notice anything that the cleared patches of earth now have in common: for example, they might all have grass seedlings. Does this mean that grass grows everywhere where there is bare earth? The children should look for links between what grows on the cleared patches and other plants growing nearby. Continued on page 64.

Developing Science
Year 5
© A & C BLACK

Down to earth: 4

Try to explain results using scientific knowledge and understanding

• **Write an explanation of the results of your investigation.**

I found that _____

_____

_____

Summarise your results in one sentence.

This could be because _____

_____

_____ ,

_____

_____

Write three possible explanations.

or _____

_____

I think the correct explanation is _____

_____

because _____

_____

_____

Give evidence to support your explanation.

Do you have enough evidence to draw a firm conclusion?

_____

_____

_____

_____

Now try this!

• **Write what else you need to do in order to draw a firm conclusion.**

Teachers' note Use this with pages 61–63. Ask the children where the seeds from which the seedlings sprouted came from. Were they already in the earth? Have they come from somewhere else? Invite the children to read out their summary and their conclusions. Ask others to question them and to try to prove them wrong, encouraging the children reading to produce evidence for their conclusions.

Developing Science
Year 5
© A & C BLACK